CREATING A CULTURE OF ACCOUNTABILITY

Gravitas Impact Monograph

MARK E. GREEN

WITH GLEN DALL

premium coaches

www.gravitasimpact.com

FOREWORD

Community. What comes to mind when you say this word out loud? Family? Friends? Colleagues? Within Gravitas Impact, "Community" has a clear and compelling meaning based on our years of experience together...the collective care, intellect and impact of members who live and are inspired by similar core values and purpose.

It is out of this community that the concept of placing our "Coach at the Center" and sharing our "Networked Intellect" has arisen. These two concepts are the genesis of the Gravitas Impact community building an ongoing series of monographs addressing important business topics, relevant to leaders worldwide who value insights in a compact and actionable format, from a deeply experienced community of professionals on six continents.

In a global business world driven by the daily media, digital marketing and "business by best seller," we have chosen to tap into the richness and robustness of our community of seasoned business leaders, coaches and thought leaders to serve those who create, build and grow one of the fundamental building blocks of secure and successful societies: the executive leadership team in a business.

If you are reading this and see a need for insight into a business challenge, please reach out to us at mongraphs@gravitasimpact.com and we would be pleased to research and potentially address it with a future monograph.

- Keith Cupp, Founder Gravitas Impact Premium Coaches

Effective execution starts with crisp accountability, and you cannot scale your business without it.

Table of Contents:

INTRODUCTION: THE VALUE OF ACCOUNTABILITY

Regardless of industry, leadership tenure, culture or geography, my coaching colleagues and I routinely observe a lack of accountability as a foundational obstacle to profitable growth and scale in small and middle-market firms. The best strategies and market opportunities in the world mean nothing if you're not able to execute your plans and get things done. *Effective execution starts with crisp accountability, and you cannot scale your business without it.*

Consider These Examples:

• At an annual planning session, the leadership team couldn't accurately recall the objectives that were set at last year's session.

• A key customer was promised delivery on a Tuesday. On Thursday morning, the angry customer called the CEO while he was out of the office.

• The CEO maintains lists of the commitments made by others in the organization to ensure nothing is forgotten.

• The executive team and staff are working very hard, but it seems like nothing meaningful is accomplished to advance the business.

• When something goes wrong, it's often difficult to ascertain who "owns" the issue, and thus who should be tasked with getting it fixed.

Now, pick just one of the above examples and contemplate the cost. It's staggering!

Maintaining crisp accountability correlates to more achievement and increases the return on investment (ROI) on your employees. Depending on industry, geography and the research you read, businesses can spend between 15-70 percent of operating expenses on employee compensation and benefits. Whatever the percentage for your particular business, the implications of increasing the return on your employee compensation expense through improved accountability are quite compelling. Aside from accomplishing more with your current staff, mastering accountability creates an environmental condition that further increases employee ROI: high performers love it and low performers hate it.

Accountability, like rigor and discipline, is virtual catnip to high-performing employees. They appreciate being held accountable and that others around them—including their leaders—are too. This creates a more predictable meritocracy in which high performers have clear objectives and the opportunity to own their results; it's a perfect environment in which to shine, stretch, feel challenged and continue to grow. As a result, they'll be even more productive and want to stay with your firm. What's more, an environment full of high performers makes it easier to attract, hire and retain other high performers.

Meanwhile, the bright light of accountability is a repellent to low-performing employees who quickly find themselves with nowhere to hide. They like to stay below the radar, blame others for their missteps and find every method possible to delay (or eliminate) the delivery of items they are required to accomplish. Clear accountability dramatically reduces a low performer's ability to practice their well-honed craft of work avoidance. Even better, it forces them to either get with the program and perform or choose the path of least resistance and quit.

As your top employees realize that the business is picking up momentum by accomplishing more while simultaneously shedding low performers, they will begin to feel an *esprit de corps* and take on a winning mentality. This is absolutely contagious and will boost the positive energy in your workplace, further accelerating the cycle.

A culture of crisp, rigorous accountability enables effective execution, retains high performers, repels low performers and improves the sense of collaboration, winning and fun in your business. This cycle drives a significantly higher employee ROI, giving you more resources and flexibility to scale—ultimately propelling you to attain your most ambitious professional and personal aspirations. With these outcomes in mind, the need to improve accountability in almost every organization is clear. **This book will show you how.**

CHAPTER 1: DEFINING ACCOUNTABILITY

What is Accountability?

accountable:
ac·count·able | *adjective*

1. Subject to giving an account: answerable
2. Capable of being explained: explainable [1]

Most notable is what's not captured in this definition: the idea of getting something done. The words *accountable* and *accountability* evoke the concept of ownership rather than accomplishment. However, the latter is generally implied through the former.

When you are required to answer, explain, and report on something, you must thoroughly understand and effectively communicate the details of what's going on. What does this look like in action? To explain this to my coaching clients, I use the practical analogy of the canary in the coal mine. In the early twentieth century, coal miners began using caged canaries to detect the presence of hazardous gasses like methane and carbon monoxide underground. If a canary died in the mine, it signified that the gas levels were toxic; an early warning system that, although unfortunate for the canaries, saved many lives.

Part of being accountable—in addition to knowing and communicating the details of what's going on—includes acting as an early warning system, much like the 'canary in the coal mine' did all those years ago. An accountable person anticipates risks in the form of obstacles, problems, and delays and shares them so that the appropriate resources can be deployed to address them before they impact the task or project at hand.

Unfortunately, some leaders don't want to hear about potential obstacles and problems; they just want to keep moving. Take note: If you shoot the messenger—or fail to employ one at all—you might stop the alarm from ringing, but you'll also ignore the danger they may alert you to and simultaneously destroy the motivation for your people to be accountable. Instead, thank them for the heads up then work together to overcome the obstacle.

At this point we've defined accountability as knowing what's happening and communicating it to others, but it's important to note that the concept of accountability is separate from the work itself—something you've likely realized if you've ever given instructions to an employee and checked in to see if they've followed through.

Being Accountable vs. Doing the Work

Although being accountable for something and actually doing the work are two separate things, quite frequently the same person is tasked with both. This is particularly true for front-line employees. For leaders and managers, accountability is commonly—but not always—separated from the work itself via delegation, similar to the way a project manager completes a project through his or her team. Problems occur when a manager delegates both accountability and doing the work to others without creating the communication channels required for the task owner to identify risks and request resources to keep themselves on track. This "fire and forget" method of assigning work is fraught with risk, prone to failure and demotivating to employees. Proper delegation formally separates tasks associated with accountability from the work itself, a critical distinction that we'll cover more deeply in chapter 5.

With these definitions and distinctions in hand, let's identify specific behaviors that are accountable and those that are not.

KEY POINTS:

What Is Accountability: An accountable person not only understands and communicates the details of what's going on—they also anticipate risks in the form of obstacles, problems, and delays and share them so that the appropriate resources can be deployed to address them before they impact the task or project at hand.

Being Accountable vs Doing The Work: Proper delegation formally separates tasks associated with accountability from the work itself.

CHAPTER 2: SYMPTOMS & BEHAVIORS

Diagnosing The Symptoms

Like experienced physicians diagnosing an illness, my coaching colleagues and I are able to diagnose an organizational accountability problem through keen observation and piecing together the symptoms. In this chapter, we'll unpack and explain the symptoms that indicate a lack of accountability, then identify specific behaviors that bolster accountability and others that undermine it.

Persistent, annoying, unresolved problems are the most common indicator of an underlying accountability deficiency. This is closely followed by a lack of progress on projects and new initiatives, and lastly, a culture of blame. These symptoms sound like: "We never seem to get anything done around here." They feel like: "We're not moving fast enough!" And they look like business leaders who are unwilling to risk conflict, challenge one another or name the elephants in the room.

Some Examples I've Seen:

- Slower-than-desired monthly financial closing and reporting.

- Missed quarterly or annual priorities due to "other things" coming up.

- Well documented, but inconsistently applied processes.

- Executive team meetings filled with "feel-good" status reporting and plausible excuse making, but absent of acknowledging the real issues and solving them.

- Executives and managers who tolerate (and often justify) underperformers.

- Routinely missed sales targets.

My coaching senses are trained to spot these frustrating conditions and then ask the CEO and the executive team one simple, powerful question: "Who is accountable for this (project, initiative, result, etc.)?" My intention is not to assign blame, but rather to have the leadership team acknowledge that a lack of clear accountability is a root cause of their problem!

An organization's symptoms do not occur in a vacuum. Human decisions and behaviors create outcomes, and there are clear, observable differences in the behaviors that lead to accountable versus non-accountable outcomes. Let's start by looking at some behaviors that contribute to a culture of accountability.

The Nine Accountable Behaviors

Maintaining Transparent Communication: You should be willing to communicate openly and honestly about the project and/or results for which you are accountable, regardless of whether the current status is good, bad or ugly. Other components of transparent communication include a 'no shame, no blame' attitude and a willingness to speak freely for the good of the project or organization.

Being Anticipatory and Pro-Active: Think multiple steps ahead of where you are rather than just focusing on what's on your plate right now. This includes contemplating second or third-order effects. For example, it's not accountable to think about a decision you must make today without considering how that decision will affect outcomes a month or a quarter from now. Every single person involved in the decision-making process should adopt the same mindset, identifying second or third-order effects and putting together plans to address them.

Remaining Results-Oriented: Business leaders—and those accountable for a particular outcome—must be very clear about what they are trying to achieve and include a mechanism to not only identify when they have reached that goal, but also measure progress along the way. When the desired results are clear, nothing is hazy or ambiguous. In addition, the team is focused on outcomes rather than activities; for example, it should be about how many sales the team has closed, not how many calls they've made in the process.

Staying Clarity-Driven: You should seek clarity in your quest to maintain accountability. What is the reality of the situation in front of you? To determine that, you must avoid rationalizing, making up stories or accepting ambiguity. Being clarity-driven is all about posing uncomfortable questions, asking for more information, making sure people are on the same page and ultimately reaching a level of detail so granular that the team can't help but have a universal understanding of progress to date, as well as where you're headed and how you'll get there.

Engaging in Disciplined Planning: You should invest a significant amount of time in planning prior to taking action. Why? Thoughtful, thorough planning provides you with the best possible chance of reaching your goals as efficiently as possible. Imagine hiring an excellent painting company to help you switch up the color of your living room. The team would likely spend 60 percent of their time just prepping the room— taping off edges, removing outlet covers, etc.—and 40 percent of it actually painting. But that preparation is the reason why their service is so great. And it's extremely accountable behavior.

Holding Yourself and Others to High Expectations: The rationale for this one is pretty simple. When you expect more, people tend to rise to the occasion and deliver. The inverse is also true: those who don't expect much usually get exactly what they bargained for. Be someone who raises the bar, rather than lowers it, and reap the corresponding benefits.

Repeating Yourself: Why is repetition a key tenet of accountability? Humans generally suck at communicating. Those delivering the message often aren't as clear as they think they are, and those on the receiving end need to hear something multiple times before they can internalize it and recognize its importance. Repeat key communications to anyone and everyone involved in achieving a particular deliverable. Don't be afraid of sounding like a broken record. In fact, your outcomes depend on it.

Continuing to Course Correct: The reality is, no matter how much you prepare, nothing goes exactly according to plan. Just as a ship has to course correct continuously to get from point A to B, so does a business. But it's far more effective to make a large number of small adjustments over time than it is to make a small number of large adjustments when you realize things aren't going the way you imagined they would. To course correct effectively, you should have continuous conversations with the members of your team who are contributing to the project to keep them on track and quickly account for any snags. When you're continuously course-correcting, you don't have to wait for a major deviation to make sure you're moving in the right direction.

Leaning In: All of these behaviors are examples of leaning in, or cultivating accountability through action. They're about maintaining a bias toward forward momentum, of anticipating and pushing for progress. Put simply, there's nothing passive about being accountable, and keeping that in mind is key to your success.

Non-accountable behaviors, on the other hand, are often passive. They tolerate team members who skate by without addressing their respective roles in hindering the project. Let's take a look at some of them now.

The Nine Non-Accountable Behaviors

Finger Pointing: Those who blame others are simply aiming to shirk their own responsibilities. Finger pointing indicates an external locus of control rather than an internal one. Instead of believing that they're responsible for a particular outcome—no matter what's happened along the way—and therefore in control and able to fix it, those who finger point are attempting to throw someone else under the bus. There's nothing accountable about that.

Withholding Information: You may think you're being a good manager, but when you don't divulge enough detail to provide your team with the depth of knowledge necessary to understand the reality of your project's condition, you're not being accountable. You're hindering everyone's ability to fulfill their part of the bargain. This could sound like: "There's a small issue, but by next week, we'll get right back on track," or, "Don't worry about it—we'll get it done." These phrases obscure the truth, and they're not at all accountable.

Letting People or Teams 'Off the Hook': We've already discussed the reality that people typically perform up to your expectations. The reverse is also true: if you continue to let people off the hook by accepting their excuses, you create a culture of mediocrity throughout your organization. It's a somewhat insidious process as well. When someone tells you they'll be caught up by next week, and you say, "Great," rather than asking how they got off track in the first place, you're setting yourself up for more excuses—and more problems—down the line.

Being Driven By Activity, Rather Than Results: I see this all the time. The pervading model in our society is that busyness is directly tied to achievement, but that's actually not true. When you focus on what you and your team are doing, rather than what you've achieved, you miss the mark. Why? In the end, all that matters is what you've actually accomplished. Knowing how much effort the team expended communicates absolutely nothing about real progress.

Putting Actions Before Plans: Like our societal tendency to prioritize busyness over actual results, maintaining a bias toward action isn't productive either. You must have clarity as to the exact direction in which you're heading to get the results you're looking for. Just think about what would happen if that same painting company we discussed came to do your bedroom, cracked the paint cans open right away, and told you that they would just try really hard not to make a mess. Would that be satisfactory to you? If not, jumping into action without a strong plan in place shouldn't be either.

Failing to Identify Clear Outcomes: We'll get into this more deeply in chapter 3, but it bears mentioning now. What happens when you don't take the time to clearly define the parameters of success and make sure everyone is on the same page? Everyone walks away from your meeting with a slightly different idea of what you're looking for. They begin working in slightly different directions. When all is said and done, it's impossible to tell whether the project has been successful or not, because everyone has a different concept of what constitutes success. This can be quite demoralizing, especially to the team doing the work. Without a clear benchmark of success, there's no finish line in sight—and there never will be.

Being Slow to Respond to Changing Conditions: If you're not responding swiftly to changing conditions, you're denying reality or pinning any progress on hope alone. Pretending that undesirable things aren't happening or wishing that everything would just work out without addressing the issues that arise just doesn't work. And it's definitely not accountable.

Communicating Infrequently: Rather than making a point of providing updates on a regular basis, you and your team may find yourselves saying, "We'll give you another update in thirty days," or sharing insights on your progress only when there's something big to report. But without a regular rhythm of transparent communication, you can't be fully accountable.

Tolerating a 'Non-Green' Status: I've been in numerous executive meetings where someone pulls up a performance dashboard filled with tasks and projects frozen in yellow. Each time, I braced myself for the reaction, waiting for someone to make a comment about all those yellow statuses being unacceptable, only to watch the whole team quickly move on to something else. That is, until I asked them why they were tolerating the lack of progress: "Why aren't you asking why everyone is off track?" My question changes the trajectory of the conversation and helps the teams better tune their expectations—and their communication—to get things unstuck. Don't let 'non-green' statuses slide; ask why things aren't moving forward and ensure plans are created to compensate.

Understanding the symptoms and behaviors associated with accountability is a critical first step in observing and acknowledging the reality of why your organization is performing below its potential. Next we'll take a long and likely uncomfortable look in the mirror to evaluate how your own behavior as a leader could be contributing to the problem.

KEY POINTS:

Diagnosing the Symptoms: Persistent, annoying, unresolved problems are the most common indicator of an underlying accountability deficiency. This is closely followed by a lack of progress on projects and new initiatives, and lastly, a culture of blame.

Accountable Behaviors: An organization's symptoms do not occur in a vacuum. Human decisions and behaviors create outcomes, and there are clear, observable differences in the behaviors that lead to accountable versus non-accountable outcomes.

Non-Accountable Behaviors: Non-accountable behaviors are often passive. Understanding the symptoms and behaviors associated with accountability is a critical first step in observing and acknowledging the reality of why your organization is performing below its potential.

CHAPTER 3: ACCOUNTABILITY STARTS WITH YOU

Leading by Example

One rainy day during the American Revolutionary War, George Washington rode up to a group of soldiers attempting to raise a massive oak beam to a high position. The corporal in charge was shouting encouragement, but the soldiers strained mightily and couldn't get the beam into position. After watching them struggle for a bit, Washington asked the corporal why he didn't join in and help, to which the corporal replied, "Don't you realize that I am the corporal?"

Very politely, General Washington replied, "I beg your pardon, Mr. Corporal, I do." Washington then dismounted his horse and worked with the soldiers to get the beam in position. When they finished, General Washington wiped the perspiration from his face, and said, "If you should need help again, call on Washington, your commander-in-chief, and I will come." [2]

George Washington lead by example, and for good reason. Whether you realize it or not, all eyes and ears within your business are focused on you. What you say and what you do are invisibly and constantly observed, scrutinized and evaluated as your managers and employees look for clues as to how they should behave. The most effective leaders I've coached consistently lead by example and walk their own talk.

Do you exhibit accountable behaviors yourself? Or do you operate from the non-accountable behavior list some (or most) of the time?

As a senior leader in the organization, you must lead by example to create the impetus for others to follow. Ask a trusted member of your team, a forum mate, or an outside professional or coach for candid feedback on whether or not you are modeling accountable behaviors on a regular basis. Identify where you need to improve and then make those changes promptly. It's crucial to do so because every shift in your organization— big or small—begins with your commitment to change yourself first! After you've addressed your behavior, you can start sizing up the rest of your team.

Right People, Right Seats

It's not uncommon for a poor accountability diagnosis to mask the probability that one (or more) members of your management team might not be the right person for their role. That is, they aren't capable of exhibiting the appropriate leadership and accountability behaviors to pull your business forward. This can be difficult to recognize and acknowledge. There is no end to the justifications you might want to offer as to why everyone on your team is 100 percent right for their role. In my nearly 20 years coaching small and mid-market leadership teams, I've heard them all.

Consider These Two Realities:

1. Your emotional attachment to longstanding members of your team interferes with your ability to objectively evaluate their performance and fit.

2. A whopping 85 percent of the leadership teams I've coached had at least one member turnover within the first twelve months of my engagement because that the person wasn't the right fit.

If you have a people problem—and the odds are you do—you have to be honest with yourself and make the switch. The wrong people in the wrong seats aren't capable of helping you improve your organization's accountability or performance. The best question to ask yourself in this regard is, "Would I enthusiastically rehire every member of my team?" Of course, the key word here is 'enthusiastically.

Raise Your Expectations

Now that you've considered your people, it's time to focus on your expectations. People perform to meet them, whatever they are. University of California psychologist Robert Rosenthal demonstrated this with an experiment that measured how teacher expectations affected student achievement. At the beginning of an academic year, Rosenthal selected children at random and informed their teachers that they had particularly high potential. Lo and behold, at the end of the school year, those "high-potential" children outperformed their peers. The explanation for their success? The teachers believed they were talented, treated them accordingly, and the students met the expectations. [3]

This phenomenon goes both ways. If the teachers had been warned that the same students were more difficult or less skilled than others, they would have changed how they related to the students and lowered their expectations. The children, in turn, probably—and unfortunately—would have met them.

An additional, extremely costly consequence of low expectations that I've observed directly in organizations is the willingness of managers to tolerate attitudes, behaviors and results that would be intolerable in a higher-expectation environment. This is not the path to crisp accountability. As you improve your own integrity as a leader, it becomes easier to hold others to the same, higher standard. You get what you expect, and both you and your people benefit from high expectations. But how do you determine exactly what to expect? Metrics.

Use Metrics

"Would you tell me, please, which way I ought to go from here?"
"That depends a good deal on where you want to get to," said the Cat.
"I don't much care where—" said Alice.
"Then it doesn't matter which way you go," said the Cat. [4]

As a leadership and growth coach, I routinely ask executive teams the same question: "At the end of the year, how will you know if the past 365 days have been successful?" Then, I take it a step further. Before they respond, I ask them to write down their answers, without talking to one another. Most of the time—the vast majority of the time, in fact—everyone in the room provides a different answer. It's an indicator that teams aren't as aligned as they think they are, nor are they as specific as they need to be when it comes to defining their goals and exactly how they'll get there. Those teams need to raise the bar on metrics. Otherwise, as the Cheshire Cat told Alice, it doesn't matter where you go if you don't care where you're going.

Ask Yourself:

- Is my team aligned on what success looks like?

- How, specifically, will we measure that concept of success?

It's been said a million times, but I'll say it again: You can't manage what you don't measure. That's why it pays to define the metrics you'll use to evaluate the business overall, functional role, key processes and progress in various projects and initiatives.

This specificity is something that's often missing for both teams and individuals at all levels of an organization. Over and over again, I see people struggle to be specific, to clearly define their desired end state or result. So, how do you get there and identify the specifics? I coach CEOs and their teams to locate the exact moment when they'll know they hit their target. For example, if a CEO's goal is to generate $2 million in net income, the exact moment she'll know she hit her target will come in the second week of January, when the CFO sends her the final numbers from the previous year, and she sees the net profit line on the P&L report.

If a sales manager is aiming to renew key customer relationships this quarter, he'll know he's accomplished that when his salesman forwards him signed sales orders or purchase agreements from those customers dated within the allotted window of time.

If you want to improve the speed and quality of a particular service you offer, you should establish specific metrics to gauge those factors and identify targets for them. You may determine if you reach or surpass a target for three months in a row, you'll have achieved that objective. The bottom line here is that until you know where you want to go, you won't be able to get there. Be specific, make sure those around you are on the same page, and see how those shifts shape your success.

As you proceed, don't forget that establishing—and maintaining—accountability in your organization begins at the top. It's up to you to get the ball rolling and keep it moving in the right direction. With that in mind, let's take a deeper dive into role accountability: making sure members of your executive team are aligned and aiming for clearly defined results so that the rest of the organization can follow their lead.

KEY POINTS:

Leading by Example: The most effective leaders I've coached consistently lead by example and walk their own talk. Do you exhibit accountable behaviors yourself? Or do you operate from the non-accountable behavior list some (or most) of the time?

Raise Your Expectations: People perform to meet your expectations, whatever they are. You get what you expect, and both you and your people benefit from high expectations.

Use Metrics: Until you know where you want to go, you won't be able to get there. Be specific, make sure those around you are on the same page, and see how those shifts shape your success.

CHAPTER 4: ROLE ACCOUNTABILITY

What is Role Accountability?

Role accountability creates clarity about the responsibilities and results associated with every seat in the business and facilitates better alignment throughout your organization. To be effective, role accountability must start at the top. In an organization, clarity and alignment only flow in one direction: down. The farther away from senior leadership you go, the fuzzier those elements become. For example, in a business with excellent clarity and alignment among the leaders, I would expect to travel down a couple of layers and find that the staff also has good clarity and alignment. When there's poor clarity and alignment at the top, by the time you reach the front lines, you're usually looking at a train wreck.

To demonstrate the downward trajectory of these crucial elements, I routinely have new clients participate in a brief exercise. I tell the CEO and executive team to, "Take five minutes and jot down a list of the results that you are paid to deliver through your role." In most cases, they can't do it. For example, the senior vice president of operations might write, "I create an environment that supports quality, get orders out on time, and monitor our success." Meanwhile, the chief talent officer may say she's paid to "recruit great employees, manage benefit functions, and develop training programs." Virtually everyone answers with verbs, not nouns—with activities rather than results.

That's the first part of the problem: most people are wired to think about actions rather than outcomes, to buy into that culture of busyness we discussed earlier. This is an issue particularly because those activities aren't measurable—at least not in a meaningful way. But the challenges only escalate from there. The exercise often reveals that there isn't a single individual accountable for each role. When more than one person is "accountable," no one is accountable. It's easy to make assumptions that things will get done, but when there's not a designated person to account for a particular result, chances are, it's not going to happen. In this kind of environment, it's also easy to point fingers—Bob thought Mary would handle it, and vice versa. Either way, the outcome is the same. Other times, we'll discover that the particular role—marketing, in this case—hasn't been filled by anyone at all; it's just implied that it will somehow get handled. Spoiler alert: it doesn't!

But the difficulties don't stop there. Next, I'll ask the CEO what results they believe each member of their executive team is paid to deliver. The items they list are almost always different than what the executives wrote down. With so much haziness at the top, there's no way that those in middle management or on the front lines have a clear sense of their roles or why they matter to the business. If that's the case in your operation, it's up to you to rectify it.

Optimizing Accountability

You can begin with the *Optimizing Accountability* tool, which helps establish role accountability for the core functions and results within your business. This tool is available for free download at **www.GravitasImpact. com/Accountability.**

Hand out the *Optimizing Accountability* tool to each member of your executive team and ask them to complete it individually. The first step is to list the names of the people accountable for each of the functions on the left-hand side of the sheet (if there are senior roles that are unique to your company, feel free to add them in the empty boxes). When everyone has finished filling out the document, share the answers. This moment, in which the entire team gets to see the lack of alignment and accountability in the organization, is often both funny and sad. But it's also a good starting point. From there, your team can work together to ensure that a single person is made accountable for each of the roles.

The next step is to determine the results and metrics for each of the core functions: What are the key outcomes and how will you measure them? The results you identify here are the appropriate answer to the question posed in the first exercise we discussed: What are the results you're paid to deliver?

Optimizing Accountability, A Client Story:

"I worked with the CEO of a private multi-location dental practice located in the Midwest. The CEO had started with one practice that they grew very successfully. They then began expanding by opening new locations around the city fairly quickly. Because the CEO couldn't be at all locations, and they were still actively involved in patients' care themselves, the practice began experiencing growth pains. There were significant issues with the culture at the new locations, which began affecting patient care, employee retention and referral rates. At one point employee turnover rates increased to 200%. The leadership team would plan and set goals, but frequently failed to achieve them. The CEO felt over-extended, frustrated and stressed at the decreasing rate of revenue growth each new location provided.

I walked the leadership team through the *Optimizing Accountability* tool as they outlined the organization's core functions, defined the necessary outcomes and indicated the accountable individuals. By doing this, we were able to visualize the gaps in accountability and highlight a major issue—the CEO was overseeing way too much. As a result, the leadership team didn't feel they had the autonomy to accomplish their goals. We also identified the need for an operations manager, someone who wasn't spending their time on services or patient care and who could oversee the offices and scheduling.

The leadership team had previously worked with consultants for planning, but there was no follow-up or accountability to the goals the leadership team made at quarterly or annual planning meetings. Now the CEO feels that, with individuals assigned to each new goal and clarity of focus through meeting cadences and tools, there is far more accountability and follow-through. The goals are met, and the CEO can already see a better quality of life for themselves, a higher-performing workplace culture and a solid foundation for future growth.

With fundamental accountability in place, a position for an operations manager, and a strategic vision for 4X growth, I'm extremely gratified that the CEO now has the freedom they deserve to grow their practice to the best it can be for them, their employees and their patients.

After our first 6 months of working together, the CEO told me, 'Glen, you should be proud of how far you've brought the team. I feel we've accomplished more in the past 6 months than we were able to in the last 7 years.' That's the power of accountability."

- Glen Dall, Gravitas Impact Coach

Accountability Cards

My follow-on assignment for clients who have completed their *Optimizing Accountability* tool is to create an Accountability Card for each role. These are different from position scorecards in that they don't capture the totality of how to be successful in a particular role; they just capture the accountability portion of it. However, we can look to the Pareto Principle—the concept that 20 percent of efforts produce 80 percent of results—to understand the importance of accountability. The two or three results that fall under the umbrella of accountability are often the most important, producing the vast majority of value for any given role.

To create the accountability cards, provide each member of your team with a 3x5 index card. Ask them to write their role at the top of the card (CFO, head of sales, etc.), and answer the question: "What are the three most important results the company expects you to deliver in exchange for paying your salary?"

That's where the fun begins, because unlike other tools which are meant to evaluate what's already there, this exercise pushes your team to get it right. They will rightly ask plenty of questions! "What do you mean by results?" or, "What if I can't measure what I do?" Reassure them that there are always measurable results; if there weren't, the company wouldn't be willing to pay their salaries. Right?

This is also the time to challenge their non-productive ingrained thought patterns—like valuing busyness—and help them narrow down their lists to capture only the results that are most valuable to the business. Once they arrive at their three most important results, they must determine how those results should be measured. For example, think back to our SVP of operations. Net profit is one of the results that role should deliver, and success is determined by how much profitability is generated: a single number. Other results may be high quality products and a safe work environment. Metrics for those may be the number of defects per thousand and the number of incidents or near misses in a set period of time, respectively.

Once the results and metrics are laid out, the next step in the process is to determine which of the three results listed is the most important. In the SVP's case, it would likely be profitability. That item should be moved to the top of the card as the lead Key Performance Indicator (KPI) for the role, and it's the KPI that needs to find its way back to the *Optimizing Accountability* tool. Note, too, that as the CEO, your role isn't exempt from this process. Your role should have a card, just like everyone else's. I'll make this easy for you, though: two of the three key results on your card should almost definitely be "right people in the right seats" and either "profitable growth" or "increase business valuation."

Once these cards are in place, there will be clarity that wasn't there before. That means it will be much easier for the executive team to stay aligned and focus on the right things. Just as we established with accountability at large, high performers love this tool—it gives them the structure and clarity necessary to deliver successfully. By the same token, low performers hate it, as it shines a spotlight on their roles and what they are (or aren't) accomplishing.

Moreover, accountability cards can—and should—be used throughout your organization. Each executive can take this process to their teams, then those leaders should conduct the exercise with their direct reports until it cascades down to every seat in the company. What if you have multiple people occupying the same role – for example, ten salespeople? Should you have ten different accountability cards? The answer is no; there should be one card—with one set of clearly defined results—for the salesperson role.

When all is said and done, any uncertainty about who is accountable for what results will be eradicated. In its place will be crisp accountability—and the employee engagement, productivity and profitability that ultimately come with it. With your roles in line, it's time to talk about process accountability: the strategies you need to actually get things done.

KEY POINTS:

What is Role Accountability? Role accountability creates clarity about the responsibilities and results associated with every seat in the business and facilitates better alignment throughout your organization.

Optimizing Accountability: You can begin with the *Optimizing Accountability* tool, which helps establish role accountability for the core functions and results within your business.

Download: www.GravitasImpact.com/Accountability.

Accountability Cards: Provide each member of your team with a 3x5 index card. Ask them to write their role at the top of the card, and answer the question: "What are the three most important results the company expects you to deliver in exchange for paying your salary?"

CHAPTER 5: PROCESS ACCOUNTABILITY

Creating an Accountability Framework

With an understanding of how to define and measure accountability, it's time to operationalize it. To ensure that everything in your organization, from large annual priorities to single tasks delegated to direct reports, gets done, you must have the right process in place. In this chapter, we'll introduce a framework, a corresponding set of rules and a simple yet powerful planning tool to operationalize and continually optimize accountability in your organization.

Creating an accountability framework begins with your expectations. As a leader who aspires to scale your business, you can't do it all. You must be able to delegate and allow others to handle various responsibilities so that you can focus on strategy and growth. This is a struggle for every leader I've coached. How do you let go while ensuring that others fulfill their part of the bargain, and to your standards? You establish accountability.

3 Building Blocks to Delegate with Accountability:

1. *Believe In Them.* If you don't believe they can accomplish the task at hand, they won't either. On the flipside, if you show them you have high expectations—that you know they can meet—those expectations become a self-fulfilling prophecy. The message comes through loud and clear, "I believe in you."

2. *Give Them the 'Why.'* Explain why the task you're assigning matters to the company and to you personally. Letting them know that you have a personal stake in it drives home the importance of what you're asking them to do.

3. *Pay Attention.* After you express how much their progress matters to you, be sure to follow up. Periodic check-ins let them know that you're watching, with full confidence they'll achieve the agreed-upon goal. [5]

The Accountability Framework in Action

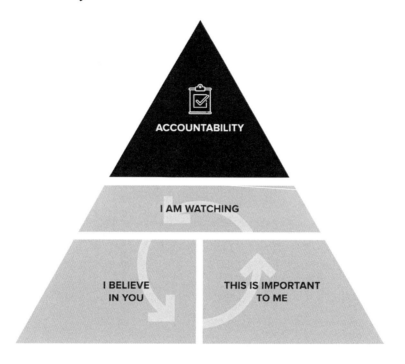

Imagine that your organization has announced its intention to integrate Core Values into every aspect of the business. To create accountability for this initiative, you would first explain that you believe everyone in the organization has the capacity to adhere to each of the company's Core Values. It may sound simplistic to you, but to your employees—people who may literally wonder whether they will have a job after your announcement—it's not simplistic at all. They need reassurances that you believe they can do it. I see CEOs miss this step all the time, which unproductively raises the collective blood pressure of the organization. Your role is to inspire them, not add to their stress.

Next, you have to explain to the organization exactly why you're doing this, and why it matters to you personally. Senior leadership is highly familiar with the concepts, books, coaching, and other background information that have led to a particular decision. In the process, you have developed a deep understanding of the importance of implementing company-wide Core Values, but the rest of the organization has not! All too often, we unconsciously assume that everyone out there has the same information we do. In most cases, they don't. You must explain why you've decided to roll out this particular initiative, including what's at stake for you personally and how adopting Core Values benefits everyone in the organization.

Finally, you must demonstrate that you're watching. This is another common point of failure. Leaders often find themselves outside of their comfort zone when talking about Core Values and so they avoid it. Don't let your discomfort stop you. I have my clients incorporate telling Core Value stories into their daily huddles. Employees share moments when they witness someone in the business living a Core Value and name the specific core value observed. It's also important to speak up when you see that Core Values aren't being upheld. When you witness behavior that doesn't align with your Core Values, have a one-on-one conversation with that employee in the moment and reference the Core Value directly. You'll reinforce the right behaviors and provide them with coaching to do better.

When the building blocks of accountability are in place, your team will have the clarity and reinforcement to know that you mean business and will do their best to meet your expectations.

Rules to Cultivate Results

In addition to the accountability framework, there are several rules that will help you stay on track. You'll remember the first rule from a previous chapter, but it bears repeating: only one person can be accountable for any particular thing. When more than one person is accountable, no one is. Keep that in mind as you assign tasks and projects to your team, and make sure other leaders in the organization follow this foundational rule.

The next rule is pretty simple: plans before actions. How do you know if you've done enough planning to move forward? A comprehensive, well thought-out plan should answer four key questions at minimum: who, why, what and when.

Who is accountable? Who are the team members that will provide support, and what are their roles in bringing the project to completion?

Why does this matter? It's crucial for the people accountable for a particular assignment, those supporting them, and the rest of the organization to understand why it matters. In answering the why, you have to be careful to go deep enough that there is real meaning behind it.

What are the clear outcomes or impact of the project, and how will you measure them? My favorite four words when working with a team in planning mode are, "as measured by what?" Make them your favorite too.

When are you going to achieve the outcomes? The answer to this one may be rather straightforward. If you're talking about a quarterly priority, you're aiming to finish it by the end of the quarter. But making sure everyone understands the target date explicitly and is on board to complete the project accordingly reinforces accountability.

The next rule is all about transparency. To ensure process accountability, the team must agree to be completely transparent with one another about everything related to what you're trying to achieve— the good, the bad and the ugly. That means you can't ever 'punish the messenger.' Instead, you should praise them, because they provide you with an extremely valuable gift: the opportunity to correct something before it becomes more of a problem. To get your employees to willingly, proactively and transparently communicate about factors that might impinge on a desired outcome, you must actively cultivate and reinforce an attitude of openness to all information.

In addition to transparency, you have to prioritize communication. Put a communication rhythm in place for each major initiative. This should be separate from the communication rhythms the organization already runs: daily huddles, and weekly, monthly and quarterly meetings. For example, the team running a particular quarterly priority may need to meet once a week on their own over the span of the quarter, so that they can be accountable by knowing, communicating and doing with focus.

If you're the one delegating a project, it may be appropriate to check in with the person accountable during your established weekly one-on-one with them, rather than setting up a separate time to discuss it. It's not always about creating a completely new meeting, sometimes it's okay to fold your project communications into an existing rhythm. What's important is to create a regular checkpoint to complete the knowing-communicating loop.

The last rule is to adopt a course-correction mentality. This one will save you an incredible amount of time, energy and money. You're much better off making continual, small course corrections to a project or behavior than you are making fewer, larger changes later on. Most of us acknowledge that there is a much higher cost associated with delayed larger corrections than with incremental ones, and yet we struggle to execute on this relatively simple idea.

There's so much fear around being labeled a micromanager that leaders miss out on real opportunities for small adjustments that yield vastly better outcomes in the end. So, face your micromanager fears head-on and address course corrections more frequently. In the end, it will be worth it!

All of this may seem straightforward, but the rules can be trickier to enact than you think. I often see CEOs trip on the same trouble spots. One of the most common issues? They don't assign a single person to be accountable; instead they give the project to the team. To avoid this mistake, clearly designate the person who will be accountable and inform the team. Another issue tends to arise with the why. Leaders simply don't provide a detailed enough explanation of the reasons behind the work. Additionally, they often fail to define the outcome well enough, which is a real problem. Recalling the Cheshire Cat's point from chapter 3: without a clear sense of the destination, it's impossible to get your team there.

Let's look at an example. A CEO declares that her company's goal is to improve customer service this quarter in order to yield happier customers. That's not very specific, and therefore not very valuable. What exactly does a 'happy customer' constitute, how do you measure that and why does it matter? Now, if she were to say that what she means by 'happier customers' is that fewer complaints result, and that fewer complaints correlate with more repeat business while also freeing more resources for innovation, the team would have more precise and useful context and clarity. A statement like that more readily translates into an achievable goal, such as, "reducing quality and service-related complaint calls by 75 percent over the next quarter." That's a specific, clear, measurable outcome. With increased context and clarity comes better results.

Priority Planning Tool

Luckily, there's a tool to facilitate this that makes process accountability easier to implement, the *Priority Planning* tool. This tool is a regular part of my coaching practice. My clients use it for quarterly and annual priority planning, but the applications for it are almost endless. I wouldn't complete this tool for something that's regularly on your to-do list, but if you're going to work on something for a month or more, or in concert with numerous other people, it's probably the right time to pull it out. The tool is configured to plan a quarterly priority with key results listed by month, but it can be modified for any time horizon. This tool is available for free download at **www.GravitasImpact.com/Accountability**.

Whoever is accountable for the project is the "owner," and should be the person completing the planning tool with input and collaboration from their team, as applicable. If you're accountable, list yourself as the "owner" for the priority and then compile your team (if applicable), listing the names of the core group helping you achieve the objective. Next, collaborate as a team to complete the planning process. What are you trying to accomplish? If your goal is to improve the on-time shipments, include that up front. Then, determine why it matters and be sure to dig deeply enough to explain exactly why it really matters.

Got all that done? Next, identify the clear measures of success, "as measured by what?" As we established, you must articulate clear, measurable outcomes. Be explicit, so that you can use a simple yes or no to indicate whether each has been achieved.

The final section of the *Priority Planning* tool to complete is the key results. The last of those results is the clear measure of success listed at the bottom of the tool. Once the planning document is completed, the owner should present it to their manager, the sponsoring executive or the leadership team at large for finalization. Everyone should agree on the clear measure of success and the explanation as to why it's important, ultimately providing a green light to proceed. This step is critical to ensure that everyone is aligned and the project team isn't moving in a direction that is different than what the sponsor or executive team intended.

KEY POINTS:

Creating an Accountability Framework: To ensure that everything in your organization, from large annual priorities to single tasks delegated to direct reports—and everything in between—gets done, you must have the right process in place.

The Accountability Framework in Action: When the building blocks of accountability are in place, your team will have the clarity and reinforcement to know that you mean business and will do their best to meet your expectations.

Rules to Cultivate Results: Who is accountable? Why does this matter? What are the clear outcomes or impact of the project, and how will you measure them? When are you going to achieve the outcomes?

Priority Planning Tool: A simple, practical, actionable tool to make it easy to implement role accountability.

Download: www.GravitasImpact.com/Accountability

CHAPTER 6: ACCELERATING ACCOUNTABILITY

The Upward Spiral of Momentum and Growth

As we conclude up our discussion of process accountability, it's time to consider how the pieces work together in a unified model: *The Upward Spiral of Momentum and Growth*. This model captures all three of the essential elements required to continually improve the accountability and capability of your people.

First, if you don't start with the right people in the right seats, which we discussed in the previous chapter, you might as well stop everything else. It's going to be a thousand times harder to accomplish anything without the right employees on board. Next, you must use the framework and rules we've introduced to create clear accountability. Once that is established, you can coach for course-correction and learning so that your people become an even more capable fit for their seats. That, in turn, improves their ability to be accountable, which elevates the level of coaching they require to grow more, and so on. The spiral continues upward, fueling itself and building momentum.

A note on coaching: it's important to coach for growth rather than for results. It's easy to fall into the trap of helping someone transactionally get things done, rather than leading them to see and address a bigger picture that includes the repeated patterns of thinking and behavior at the root of their challenges. This is where growth, development and increased capability occur.

When you coach your people, have them look at the patterns that hold them back. What could they have done differently? This is far more effective to increase capability than solving the problem for them just to get the work done. It's tempting to coach for results because you tend to get them. Your efforts close the sale or finish the project, but employees don't really learn or grow. And unfortunately, their capabilities don't spiral up over time or strengthen the system in any way. But when you coach for growth, it's an entirely different story.

One of my clients, a $75 million manufacturing company, had a significant accountability problem when it came to research and development (R&D). After completing the role accountability process discussed in chapter 4, it became clear that no one person was accountable for R&D. This was a serious problem, because the company's strategy was driven by innovation. But with a bright light now shining on the problem, we could make progress. The solution was to get the right person in the right seat, so the CEO hired a director of R&D and created a very clear accountability card and scorecard for the role.

Over time, it became apparent that the new director was capable, but was challenged influencing and working with other leaders due to her personal style. The CEO began to worry whether the director was, in fact, the right person in the right seat. But because of the CEO's familiarity with the *Upward Spiral of Momentum and Growth*, he began providing the director of R&D specific, growth-oriented, course-corrective coaching. It took a bit longer than anyone would have liked, but the director eventually turned the corner and became a terrific fit for her role and a model team player.

Their R&D engine is now humming along with better results than the company had ever achieved in its history. And this director, who many feared wasn't the right person for the seat, was successfully coached up the spiral to be exactly who the company needed her to be to drive their R&D capabilities forward. Although this company experienced the business equivalent of a fairytale ending to their R&D story, there's more to this than checking boxes and employing tools. Behind the scenes, the CEO was also coached to stretch and grow so that he could be accountable and do the work that was required. Like my client, you must lead your team's path up the spiral of momentum and growth by example.

Deliberate Practice

Unless you're scaling a psychology practice or a training and development firm, you're probably not in the business of behavior change—and yet, you must be. Throughout this monograph, you've seen that a high accountability organization requires every member of your team—from the C-suite to the front lines—to adjust both their thinking and their actions. It's your job to help them change, and that's not necessarily easy.

Leading behavioral change—like my client's journey up the spiral— is inherently challenging. It will push you beyond your comfort zone, as all real progress does. Think about how you learned to ride a bike or perhaps speak a second language. You felt out of your element, but it was part of the process required to grow your capability. Now you'll need to embrace discomfort and some organizational pain rather than succumbing and retreating, and help others do the same.

How do you cultivate progress toward change in yourself? Deliberate practice—a concept identified by psychologists K. Anders Ericsson, Ralf Krampe, and Clemens Tesch-Römer. They studied how those at the very top of their field got there and what dictated their success. The researchers found that it wasn't innate talent. Rather, it was what they labeled deliberate practice, or "effortful activity designed to optimize improvement." That effortful activity helped the experts they studied...grow into experts.[6]

Deliberate practice will help you advance up the spiral in terms of your ability to be accountable and to hold others to the same high standard. To get started, first pick the accountable behavior from chapter 2 that you most want to improve. Next, ask a member of your team or a trusted peer to provide you with feedback on how you're doing. Then begin practicing.

Three Key Elements to Deliberate Practice:

• Motivation to stretch one's capabilities.

• Extreme repetition.

• Flow of feedback.

Although the feedback you'll get through deliberate practice is crucial, there's another element you can add to generate additional ideas regarding how to implement the accountable behavior you selected. In his book *What Got You Here Won't Get You There: How Successful People Become Even More Successful,* Marshall Goldsmith introduces the concept of 'feedforward.' Feedforward is an easy-to-implement process to solicit ideas about how to accomplish something.

For example, if holding yourself and others to the highest expectations is the accountable behavior you'd like to improve, seek feedforward by talking to three or four people who might have ideas to help you. Ask them, "What are some things that would help me get better at holding myself and others to higher expectations?" Then listen carefully and write down what they say. Reach out to your peers, to a coach or trusted advisor, and to selected members of your team. Once you have their insights on how to move forward, implement the small number of ideas that you believe would work best for you. Be sure to use deliberate practice as you do.

Accelerating Your Results

If you're like the vast majority of CEOs I know, you're concerned with speed, which means you're probably thinking "How long will this process take?" Your velocity and advancement up the spiral will be determined by how you go about the work. The bottom line: if you put in the work, one way or another, you'll get the results you seek over time. But often, employing an expert can dramatically accelerate your process.

The Three Steps To Accelerate Your Results:

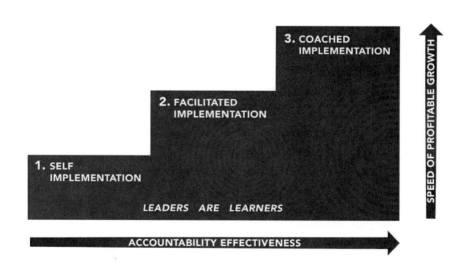

When you do it yourself, or self-implement, you already have all of the resources you'll utilize at your fingertips and there are no hard-dollar costs for outside expertise associated with your efforts. But there are downsides, too. Ascending the spiral could take a lot longer than you hope, and you won't necessarily have the expertise you need to implement changes effectively. You may also incur significant soft-dollar costs due to the opportunity cost of deploying resources at the expense of other initiatives, potential delays and lack of efficiency, which could more than offset any hard-dollar savings.

The next step is a facilitated workshop by a trained professional to work through the thinking, tools and behavioral changes discussed in this monograph. A workshop for your team will accelerate your progress up the spiral through more rapid implementation of the tools and adoption of more rigorous accountability within the organization. There's less of a time commitment necessary from your team, and it will save you the effort of having to backtrack and redo things you may not have executed properly on your own. Although there are certainly hard-dollar costs to engage a facilitator, the payback is vastly accelerated progress.

Finally, you could choose to fully engage a coach—a qualified expert who works closely with your leadership team throughout the year in a monthly rhythm. The benefits here? Beyond the domain of accountability, you'll systemically address the leadership, talent, strategy, execution, profit, customer and systems issues necessary to more profitably and sustainably scale your firm.

With a coach by your side, you'll also benefit from the time and energy savings associated with expert pattern recognition. You'll have an expert on your team to recommend strategies based on their experience seeing similar patterns play out in numerous organizations as they scale. It's the same mechanism by which a chess master is able to see the right move as soon as they look at the board, whereas less experienced players see a number of potential moves and are unsure of which would be best. The costs associated with this step include a larger commitment of funding, time, focus, and energy.

Although one could argue that you should be investing the same amount of time, focus and energy in your business's growth anyway, with a qualified coach, you'll be significantly more effective, generating a return on investment well beyond their fees. Over the years, I've met many CEOs who began a change initiative with self-implementation, only to engage an outside expert later on. In each of these situations, the universal reaction after the fact is a wistful acknowledgment that they should have hired a professional from the start. Though it was certainly more expensive than the DIY approach, they realized it was much more effective and efficient to work with an expert who could accelerate their learning and growth.

If you'd like to explore any of these next steps to accelerate your progress, Gravitas Impact can help. Visit **www.GravitasImpact.com** or call **877-217-2253** to start the conversation.

Accountability in Action

Regardless of what you've achieved in the past or where you're heading in the future, increasing accountable behaviors in yourself and your team will accelerate the achievement of your goals. At the same time, you must be mindful of how the spiral works: start with the right people in the right seats, continually elevate their accountability and provide course-correcting, growth-oriented coaching. The absence of any one of those leads to a frustrating oscillation as you and your people move around the spiral, only to slide back to where you started.

But once you get it right and create bar-raising accountable behaviors in yourself and others, you'll reap the fruits of your labor in the form of more effective execution, increased retention of high performers, fewer low performers and an energetic *esprit de corps* throughout the organization. All of this yields a higher ROI per employee, accelerated growth and more value in the business. Best of all, you'll have less stress, more fun, and more time to truly enjoy the journey toward your highest aspirations.

KEY POINTS:

The Upward Spiral of Momentum and Growth: This model captures all three of the essential elements required to continually improve the accountability and capability of your people. The spiral continues upward, fueling itself and building momentum.

Deliberate Practice: Deliberate practice will help you advance up the spiral in terms of your ability to be accountable and to hold others to the same high standard.

Accelerating Your Results: If you'd like to explore any of these next steps to accelerate your progress, Gravitas Impact can help.

Visit **www.GravitasImpact.com** or call **877-217-2253** to start the conversation.

Accountability in Action: Regardless of what you've achieved in the past or where you're heading in the future, increasing accountable behaviors in yourself and your team will accelerate the achievement of your goals.

DOWNLOAD YOUR FREE

ACCOUNTABILITY TOOLS AT

www.GravitasImpact.com/Accountability

Notes

1 - Merriam-Webster Dictionary Online, "Accountable." https://www.merriam-webster.com/dictionary/accountable (2019).

2 - Maxwell, John C. The 5 Levels of Leadership: Proven Steps to Mazimize your Potential. NY Center Street Press, 2011.

3 - Rosenthal, Robert and Jacobson, Lenore. "Teacher Expectations for the Disadvantaged," Scientific American 218 (1968).

4 - Carroll, Lewis. Alice's Adventures in Wonderland. Peterborough, Ont.: Broadview Press, 2000.

5 - Green, Mark E. Activators – A CEO's Guide to Clearer Thinking and Getting Things Done. Warren, NJ, 2018.

6 - K. Anders Ericsson, Ralf Krampe, and Clemens Tesch-Römer, "The Role of Deliberate Practice in the Acquisition of Expert Performance," Psychological Review, vol. 100, no. 3 (1993).

Recommended Reading:

Topgrading, Bradford Smart: Evaluate your existing team and modify your hiring practices to get the right people in the right seats.

WHO, Geoff Smart and Randy Street: Avoid hiring mistakes and attract A players to your company.

Measure What Matters, John Doerr: Clarify your measurable key results and understand the power of creating measurable objectives.

The 3x5 Coach, Dave Baney: Delve more deeply into accountability cards and their effectiveness.

Activators, Mark E. Green: Close the gap between the leader you are and the leader you aspire to become.

What Got You Here Won't Get You There, Marshall Goldsmith: Keep yourself accountable with the process of creating "feedforward."

ABOUT THE AUTHOR:

Mark E. Green is a business and leadership growth coach to CEOs and executive teams worldwide. He has addressed, coached and advised thousands of business leaders, helping them unlock more of their potential and teaching them how to do the same for their teams.

Mark's first book *Activators – A CEO's Guide to Clearer Thinking and Getting Things Done* exposes the unconscious mechanisms that interfere with your thinking and results and provides proven guidance and easy-to-use tools to help you and your teams accomplish more.

His integrity, direct style and powerful intuition accelerate team performance, distribution of decision-making, productivity, revenue and profitability. Mark's clients report significantly lower stress, reduced time consumed by the business and vastly improved quality of life.

He is a Core Advisor to Gravitas Impact Premium Coaches, a mentor to coaches worldwide, and an active contributor to programs and content for their global ecosystem.

CONTACT MARK: www.mark-green.com

Glenn Dall is a successful CEO with an inspiring personal story and hard-won experience stepping in to lead the turnaround and growth of a publicly-traded company. Today Glen is the founder and leader of Apex North Business Coaching, dedicated to helping others grow their careers and companies Apex North picks up where consultants, business groups, and frameworks like EOS leave off.

ABOUT GRAVITAS IMPACT:

WHO WE ARE:

Gravitas Impact is a vibrant community of experienced business coaches across the globe devoted to helping you achieve your extraordinary goals.

WHAT WE DO:

Gravitas Impact pairs companies with the most experienced, effective executive coaches in the world. Our coaches use time-tested tools and concepts to guide leadership and executive teams towards dramatically improving their organizational performance, revenue and culture.

Our coaches and their clients appreciate knowing that we set a high bar for acceptance into our organization. These premium coaches bring their clients the most current and incisive expertise, based on constantly updated insights and tools from our events, trainings and network of faculty thought leaders. From world-class intellectual property in multiple languages, to time-tested growth concepts and tools, Gravitas Impact offers coaches access to ongoing, continuous education and training in tools from thought leaders and guest speakers.

BECOME A COACH: www.GravitasImpact.com/Apply

FIND A COACH: www.GravitasImpact.com/Hire

BEST COMMUNITY – BEST LEARNING – BEST TOOLS

Made in the USA
Las Vegas, NV
26 October 2022